Simple Animal Coloring Fun Relaxation

By Jesse Buenoano

Published by PUBLISHING COMPANY in 2019
First edition: First printing
Illustrations and design 2019 Jesse Buenoano

ISBN 9781691979264

Coffee

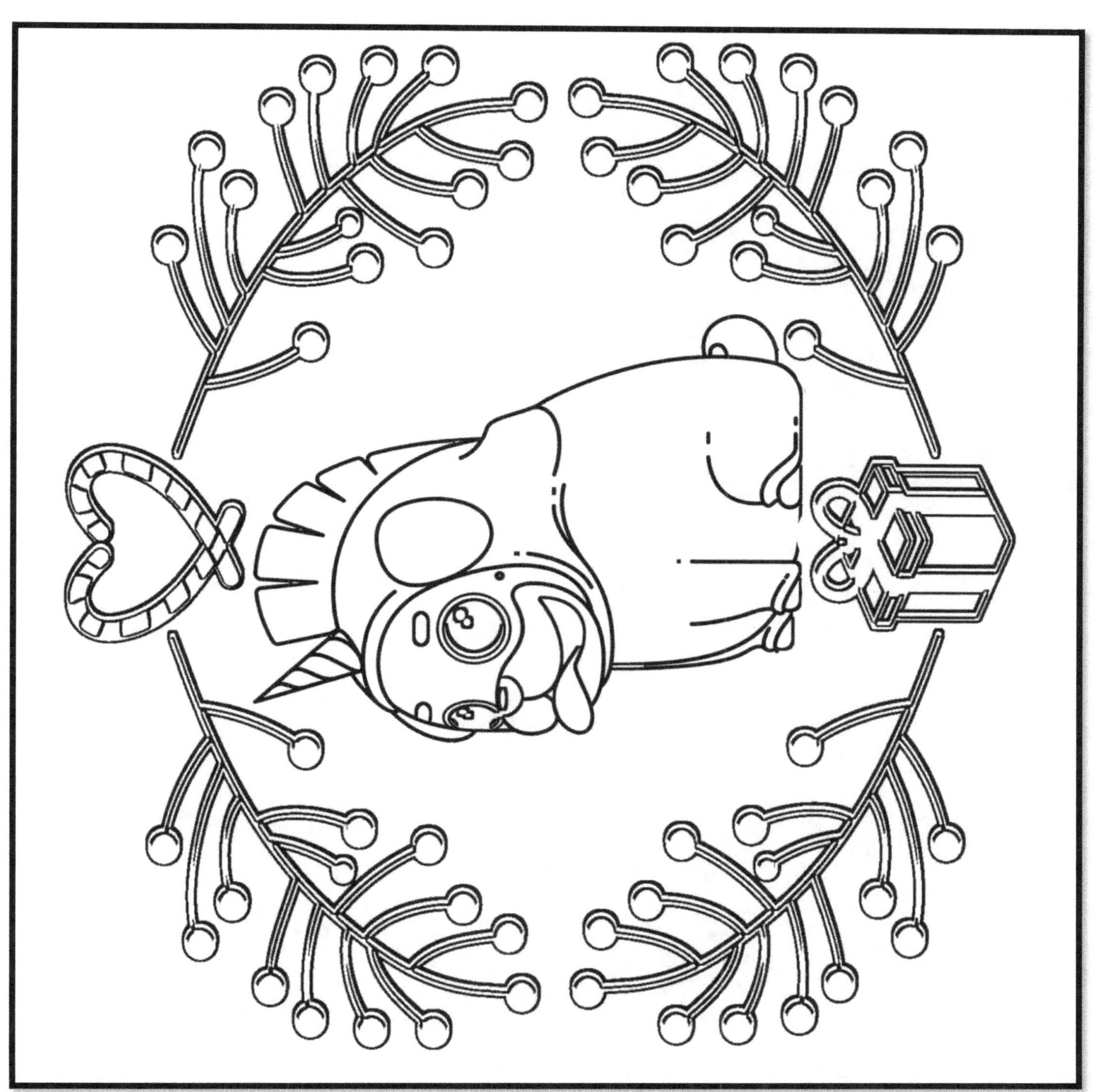

www.ingramcontent.com/pod-product-compliance
Lightning Source LLC
Chambersburg PA
CBHW081630250726
48657CB00009B/2815